I0428828

TABLE OF CONTENTS

Foreword   3

Introduction   5

    I. Voting Rights   7

    II. Education   12

    III. Employment Discrimination   17

    IV. Fair Housing   21

    V. Public Accommodations   25

    VI. Policing the Police and Prosecuting the Klan   28

Recommendations   32

Conclusion   41

INTRODUCTION

My friends, to those who say that we are rushing this issue of civil rights, I say to them we are 172 years late.
                    Vice President Hubert H. Humphrey, 1948[2]

Until the late nineteenth century, African Americans in the United States, particularly in the American South, were regarded both politically and socially as second-class citizens. Though the 13th, 14th, and 15th Amendments to the Constitution had been ratified, they were not being implemented with the full force of the law. Moreover, the courts and the federal government had nullified much of the Reconstruction-era Civil Rights Acts.[3]

In 1939, the Justice Department established a Civil Rights Section within its Criminal Division for criminal prosecutions of peonage and involuntary servitude cases, as well as for prosecutions under the remaining Civil Rights Acts.[4] The Section was given limited authority and a small staff. Fighting a World War against Nazism, however, made it increasingly difficult for the United States to defend racial discrimination within its own borders, especially while African-American troops were committed to the struggle for anti-discrimination abroad. The return of Black veterans to the home front provided local leadership and a political framework for civil rights protest that the federal government could no longer ignore.

President Truman established a Committee on Civil Rights in 1946. Its 1947 report, *To Secure These Rights*, recommended comprehensive civil rights legislation as well as the creation of a Civil Rights Division within the Justice Department.[5] Although President Eisenhower did not embrace civil rights as a political priority within the Administration, Attorney General Herbert Brownell advocated additional governmental efforts. Brownell collaborated with civil rights organizations, including the Leadership Conference on Civil Rights, to propose a civil rights bill that would require both civil remedies and criminal penalties for civil rights violations.

---

[2] Humphrey, Hubert H. "1948 Democratic National Convention Address" (1948). Available at: http://www.americanrhetoric.com/speeches/huberthumphey1948dnc.html

[3] The Justice Department was limited to criminal prosecutions under these statutes. From the Civil War to 1940, the Justice Department brought only two prosecutions for racial violence, one in 1882 and one in 1911.

[4] In addition to civil rights cases, the Civil Rights Section was also responsible for administering the criminal provisions of the Fair Labor Standards Act, the Safety Appliance Act, the Hatch Act, and certain other statutes. It also processed most of the mail received by the federal government relating to civil rights issues.

[5] The Truman Committee believed that increasing the level of federal civil rights enforcement from a Section within the Criminal Division to its own separate Division "would give the federal civil rights enforcement program prestige, power, and efficiency that it now lacks." President Truman's Committee on Civil Rights, *To Secure These Rights*, 152.

On September 9, 1957, President Dwight Eisenhower signed the Civil Rights Act of 1957, the first civil rights legislation since Reconstruction. While the Act could not implement everything necessary to protect the political, social, and economic rights of African Americans, it did authorize three important features: a position for an Assistant Attorney General for Civil Rights within the Department of Justice; the creation of the United States Commission on Civil Rights; and the use of civil suits against voting discrimination.

On December 9, 1957, Attorney General William P. Rogers signed AG Order No. 155-57, formally establishing the Civil Rights Division of the Department of Justice. In the 50 years since its creation, the Division has been instrumental in promoting equal justice for all Americans.

The following report discusses the efforts of the Civil Rights Division over the past 50 years to eliminate discrimination in the areas of education, employment, housing, voting, criminal justice, and public accommodations. We provide the historical context for the Division's involvement in each area, outline the Division's landmark achievements, and assess the challenges it currently faces in securing equal and impartial administration of justice under the law. Finally, we provide recommendations for the Division to consider as it sets out to achieve its mission of effective civil rights enforcement over the next 50 years. We invite the Division, Congress, and the public to examine and reflect on this report as a piece of an ongoing dialogue regarding how best to secure and protect the civil rights of the American people.

I. VOTING RIGHTS

*We cannot, we must not, refuse to protect the right of every American to vote...
But even if we pass this bill, the battle will not be over. What happened in Selma
is part of a far larger movement which reaches into every section and State of
America...It is all of us, who must overcome the crippling legacy of bigotry and
injustice. And we shall overcome.*
President Lyndon Baines Johnson, 1965[6]

In 2004 and 2005, *Forbes* magazine ranked Secretary of State Condoleezza
Rice the most powerful woman in the world. A Phi Beta Kappa at age 19, with a
doctorate degree in the politics of the former Soviet Union, she was the first
female, first minority, and youngest Provost at Stanford University before serving
in President George H.W. Bush's administration as Soviet and East European
advisor. She served the current President Bush first as National Security Advisor
and then Secretary of State. As the first African-American woman and the
second woman ever to head the United States Department of State, Secretary
Rice's race and gender are always noted but rarely invoke surprise. But 50
years ago, an African-American Secretary of State, from Birmingham, Alabama,
would have been impossible.

In mid-twentieth century America, African Americans were regarded both socially
and politically as second-class citizens. Prior to the Civil War, Blacks were
disenfranchised throughout the states – Blacks in the South were still enslaved
and their Northern counterparts were, for the most part, denied the rights of
citizenship. Latino voters faced similar barriers to voting in Texas and other parts
of the Southwest, as did Native American and Asian-American voters in the
West. Fifty years ago, the vast majority of Blacks living in the South, like
Secretary Rice's parents in Birmingham, Alabama, were barred from voting.

Americans born after the civil rights era of the 1960s may find it difficult to
imagine that there was ever a period in which advocating the right to vote for
African Americans and other racial minorities provoked controversy. Yet, in
Alabama and throughout the South, it generated widespread hostility and even
violence. In 1963, Birmingham Police Commissioner Eugene "Bull" Connor
ordered police to open fire hoses on hundreds of young, nonviolent Blacks – both
children and adults – who were protesting for their civil rights. Later that year,
members of the Ku Klux Klan planted a dynamite bomb in the basement of
Birmingham's 16th Street Baptist Church, a center for those resisting segregation
and demanding the vote. The explosion killed four young girls, including one of
Secretary Rice's classmates – 11-year old Denise McNair.

---

[6] President Lyndon B. Johnson. Speech Before Congress on Voting Rights. 15 March 1965.
Available at:
http://millercenter.virginia.edu/scripps/digitalarchive/speeches/spe_1965_0315_johnson?print

Far from intimidating the Black community and its many supporters, the deaths of innocent children shocked the nation and the world. Then, in March 1965, on a bridge outside Selma, Alabama, civil rights activists, led by Dr. Martin Luther King, Jr., and others, took to the streets in a peaceful protest for voting rights. They were met with clubs and violence. Many were beaten and severely injured, including a young activist named John Lewis – now Congressman Lewis. But the activists did not march in vain. Television brought this conflict of angry violence against peaceful, moral, protest into living rooms across America. Five days later, President Johnson announced to a joint session of Congress that he would bring them an effective voting rights bill. Echoing the spiritual anthem of the civil rights movement, he said simply, "We shall overcome." Shortly thereafter, Congress passed the Voting Rights Act.

This landmark legislation, called the most effective civil rights law ever enacted, would not have passed without the stirring words of Martin Luther King, Jr., the daily local struggles of civil rights activists, and the congressional arm-twisting of President Johnson. But it was the early cases under the 1957 and 1960 Civil Rights Acts, brought both by the Civil Rights Division and a core of private civil rights lawyers, that ultimately shaped the contents of the 1965 Voting Rights Act.[7]

From 1960 to 1964, Division attorneys traveled throughout the South to investigate voting discrimination and compiled overwhelming evidence of inequity. In a county-by-county and state-by-state campaign in Alabama, Georgia, Louisiana, and Mississippi, the Division challenged voting discrimination in federal courts. The Division faced hostile judges, defiant state and local officials, and widespread tactics of violence and intimidation toward Blacks attempting to register to vote.

In statewide cases against Louisiana and Mississippi in 1961 and 1962, respectively, the Civil Rights Division argued that some state laws were designed with discriminatory intent while others had the effect of preventing Blacks from voting. In Mississippi, for example, state provisions required Blacks applying to vote to copy and interpret provisions of the state constitution to the satisfaction of the White registrars, which allowed them to summarily deny qualified Black residents the opportunity to register. In Louisiana, District Judge John Minor Wisdom ruled that parishes could no longer give Blacks any tests more onerous than those that had previously been given to Whites – which generally meant no tests at all.[8] The Supreme Court upheld the decision, ruling that a court not only has "the power but the duty to render a decree which will, so far as possible, eliminate the discriminatory effects of the past as well as bar like discrimination in the future."[9]

---

[7] See Landsberg, Brian K. *Free at Last to Vote: The Alabama Origins of the 1965 Voting Rights Act.* Lawrence: University Press of Kansas, 2007.
[8] *United States. v. Louisiana*, 225 F. Supp. 353 (E.D. La. 1963), aff'd 380 U.S. 145 (1965).
[9] *United States. v. Louisiana*, 380 U.S. 145 (1965).

Even when the Division obtained favorable rulings from some federal judges, striking down discriminatory voting practices, new barriers were quickly put into place. Those struggling for voting equality could not keep up with those fighting against it. The limits of the 1957 and 1960 Civil Rights Acts and the inability of the Division's case-by-case litigation to secure and enforce the necessary changes to local practices, pushed Congress to consider more rigorous, ground-breaking provisions in the final voting rights bill, including Section 5 of the Act, which required states and counties with the most egregious histories of entrenched discrimination against minority voters to have their voting changes pre-approved by the federal government before they could be implemented. The Act also prohibited discrimination against racial minorities in voting and authorized the Department of Justice to appoint federal examiners to register voters where local officials refused and to monitor whether elections were being conducted fairly. Civil Rights Division lawyers, particularly Harold Greene – who later became a federal judge in D.C. – drafted the initial proposal and language to be included in the final version of the Voting Rights Act.

On August 6, 1965, the day President Johnson signed the Voting Rights Act into law, he directed the Attorney General to file suit against the Mississippi poll tax.[10] The Attorney General immediately sent letters to every county registrar in every state covered by the Voting Rights Act to note the Act's suspension of discriminatory devices previously used to bar Blacks from voting. The following week, the Civil Rights Division brought poll tax suits against Texas, Alabama, and Virginia, and federal examiners were dispatched to 14 counties to register Black voters. During that first week alone, federal examiners registered over 15,000 Blacks, and another 27,000 by the end of the first month.[11] As of June 30, 1966, over 117,000 African Americans were registered by federal examiners in Alabama, Mississippi, Louisiana, and South Carolina. Within 10 years of passing the Voting Rights Act, Black registration in the Deep South had increased by over 1 million people.

The priorities of the Civil Rights Division's Voting Section have shifted periodically since passage of the Voting Rights Act, concurrent with Supreme Court interpretations of its meaning. The Supreme Court ruled in 1969, for instance, that all voting changes in covered jurisdictions – including redistricting and reapportionment – were subject to Section 5 preclearance; is also ruled in 1973 that the 14th Amendment prohibited "vote dilution."[12] In light of these decisions, the range of objections the Voting Section could raise – which subsequently included all voting changes with a discriminatory purpose or effect – became a powerful lever in prodding many jurisdictions to abandon at-large election systems, discriminatory annexations, and racial gerrymandering.

---

[10] Twice earlier, in 1937 and in 1951, the Supreme Court had upheld the poll tax as constitutional. It overruled these cases in 1965 in *Harper v. Virginia*, 383 U.S. 663 (1965).
[11] In the first year after the Act went into effect, the Attorney General dispatched examiners to 43 counties and observers to another 23.
[12] *White v. Register*, 412 U.S. 775 (1973).

In 1980, however, the Supreme Court dealt voting rights enforcement a significant setback. In *City of Mobile v. Bolden*,[13] the Court held that in order to prove voting discrimination under Section 2 of the VRA, the plaintiff had to show that the policy or procedure in question was motivated by a discriminatory purpose. This temporarily limited the range of election practices to which the Voting Section could legally object. Thankfully, when it renewed the Voting Rights Act in 1982, Congress overturned the *Bolden* ruling, making clear that it is unnecessary to prove that certain registration and voting practices have been established with discriminatory intent. Instead, a Section 2 violation occurs if a court concludes that a voting practice has the *effect* of discriminating against minority voters, whether or not it was motivated by bias. The re-establishment of the discriminatory "results" test as the standard for bringing a Section 2 challenge again allowed the Civil Rights Division to intervene more effectively to combat discriminatory election policies.

From the late 1970s through the 1980s, the Section 5 preclearance requirement and the Voting Section's litigation under Section 2 of the Voting Rights Act curbed efforts to dilute minority voting strength. Following both the 1980 Census and the 1990 Census, Division efforts yielded remarkable gains in the ability of minority voters to participate in the political process. After the 1990 Census and the resulting round of redistricting, the number of Black and Latino representatives in Congress and in state houses across the country increased dramatically. Intervening when redistricting had a discriminatory purpose or effect has made voters increasingly able to elect candidates of their choice at every level of government.[14]

While some voting enforcement has continued in recent years, most notably to ensure that the minority language provisions of the Act – Sections 203 and 4(f)(4) – are vigorously prosecuted, much of the core work of the Voting Section has been significantly diminished. In the last several years, the Section has brought only a handful of Section 2 cases on behalf of African Americans, Hispanics, Asian Americans, and Native Americans. Though Congress added the National Voter Registration Act (NVRA) – also known as the "Motor-Voter" bill[15] – to the Civil Rights Division's enforcement arsenal in 1993, the Section has been pressing states to purge the voter rolls rather than ensure that states allow registration at social service agencies. Moreover, in pursuing the newest voting legislation, the Help America Vote Act (HAVA), a political appointee in the Division urged Arizona to apply the most cramped interpretation. This restrictive view of the new law would have limited voters' opportunities to use provisional

---

[13] 446 U.S. 55 (1980).

[14] See *Busbee v. Smith*, 549 F. Supp. 494 (1982), regarding Georgia's legislative redistricting in 1981. See *Garza v. County of Los Angeles*, 756 F. Supp. 1298 (C.D. Cal. 1990), regarding Section 2 litigation in L.A. County that resulted in the creation of a Hispanic majority district and the first Hispanic County Commissioner in 1992.

[15] The NVRA requires states to provide voter registration materials to departments of motor vehicles and offices that provide public assistance and/or disability benefits.

ballots, thus defying the position of the Election Assistance Commission, which has the principle role in implementing HAVA.

Ensuring the voting rights of all Americans in the twenty-first century demands more innovative tactics and approaches than were required during the period of overt segregation and racial discrimination. The Civil Rights Division, in changing its approach, must not stray from its original mission to ensure political equality.

II. EDUCATION

The plurality's postulate [in the recent Supreme Court decision regarding school desegregation efforts in Seattle and Louisville] that 'the way to stop discrimination on the basis of race is to stop discriminating on the basis of race,'...is not sufficient...To the extent the plurality opinion suggests the Constitution mandates that state and local school authorities must accept the status quo of racial isolation in schools, it is, in my view, profoundly mistaken.
Justice Kennedy, *Parents v. Seattle School Dist. No. 1*[16]

The school bell rings at T.C. Williams High School in Alexandria, Virginia. A group of students from Mr. Harrison's Advanced Placement Government class pours out into the hall, discussing last week's basketball game against West Potomac. The cafeteria boasts a racially, ethnically, and socioeconomically diverse scene. Of the two thousand students enrolled at T.C. Williams, a quarter is Hispanic, a quarter is White, and forty-three percent are Black. Dozens of flags exemplifying the student body's diversity of nationality hang in the school lobby; meanwhile, the city's payment for its students' AP exams and T.C. Williams' initiative to provide every student with a laptop confirm its commitment to leveling the playing field for its students of diverse socioeconomic backgrounds.[17]

The diversity of Mr. Harrison's class, while perhaps not typical, was unimaginable 50 years ago in Virginia. Efforts to racially integrate public schools in Virginia have been met with periods of widespread resistance since the Civil War. While many school districts employed tactics to stall integration and to avoid questions as to the racial equality of their facilities, perhaps nowhere was massive resistance more successfully employed than in 1950s Prince Edward County, Virginia. Recounting the story of Prince Edward County sheds light on the progress that has been made regarding issues of educational equality over the past 50 years and, more importantly, the civil rights work in public education that remains our business to resolve.

Prince Edward County is located in a Southside area of Virginia in the region known 50 years ago as the "Black Belt."[18] Stretching from the shores of the Chesapeake Bay down south through the Carolinas and Georgia and west toward East Texas, the counties in that region were predominantly rural and at least one-third Black. Each one embraced stringent laws and social norms enforcing the separation of the races. In 1939, Robert Russa Moton High School was constructed for Blacks in Prince Edward County in an attempt to avoid legal challenge from the NAACP regarding inadequate educational facilities. The new

---

[16] *Parents Involved in Community Schools v. Seattle School Dist. No. 1*, 127 S. Ct. 2738 (2007); Kennedy, J., concurring.
[17] "T.C. Williams High School Profile." *Alexandria City Public Schools* (2007); Available at: www.acps.k12.va.us/profiles/tcw.php; www.en.wikipedia.org/wiki/T._C._Williams_High_School.
[18] *Prince Edward County: The Story Without An End—A Report Prepared for the U.S. Commission on Civil Rights*. July 1963; Available at www.library.vcu.edu/jbc/speccoll/pec03a.html.

school, however, was overcrowded and underfunded – it lacked a gymnasium, cafeteria, desks, lockers, restrooms, and an auditorium with seats. When the school's repeated requests for additional funds were denied by the all-white school board, students at R.R. Moton took matters into their own hands.

In 1951, some 450 students walked out of the school in protest against the educational conditions in Black Prince Edward schools. Supported by the Richmond NAACP, the students' case, *Davis v. County School Board of Prince Edward County*, became one of the five cases combined under the name *Brown v. Board of Education* in the 1952-1953 Supreme Court term. This decision, which overturned *Plessy v. Ferguson* (1896) and declared racial segregation to be unconstitutional, was met with massive resistance in Prince Edward County. Since the Supreme Court specified no time frame for desegregation in *Brown I* (1954), local White leadership delayed its implementation and organized plans to underwrite White teacher salaries to insure that quality White education would continue untouched. Following the 1957 decision in *Brown II* that schools must desegregate "with all deliberate speed," the Prince Edward County school board epitomized Virginia's recalcitrant policy of massive resistance in its 1959 decision to close its doors to all public education.

Though the county government refused to appropriate funds for the public school system, various organizations raised money for White families to send their children to private or parochial schools. In 1961, the State of Virginia allocated funds for tuition grants and tax concessions for White children to go to private segregated schools, while Black children were either denied public education or forced to relocate to other counties. It wasn't until 1964 in the Supreme Court case *Griffin v. County School Board* that Prince Edward County's and the State of Virginia's actions were declared unconstitutional. County schools were subsequently ordered to reopen and to integrate.

In 1964, only 1.2 percent of Black students in the entire South attended schools with Whites. In reaction to the dismal state of racial integration throughout the South, Congress passed the Civil Rights Act of 1964. A comprehensive measure mandating nondiscrimination in public education, facilities, accommodations, employment, and federally assisted programs, the Act authorized the Justice Department to intervene in race-based equal protection cases.[19] Though the Civil Rights Division was not a plaintiff in the *Brown v. Board* or the *Griffin* litigation, Title IV of the 1964 Act authorized the Department thenceforth to bring suit against racial segregation. Additionally, Title VI dictated that federal agencies, including the Department of Health, Education, and Welfare, be responsible for ensuring nondiscrimination in federally funded programs – including public schools. The Act also provided for rescinding federal funds for noncompliance.

---

[19] Congress also included national origin, sex, and religion in the categories of people to whom equal protection under the Civil Rights Act of 1964 would extend.

In 1966 alone, the Civil Rights Division brought 56 school desegregation cases under Title IV, Title VI, and Title IX.[20] The Department challenged the legitimacy of dual school systems throughout the South and endeavored to equalize facilities while integrating teaching staff, school activities, and athletics. The decisions resulting from cases brought by the Civil Rights Division required that the school systems not only allow Black children to attend previously all-white schools, but that they "undo the harm" created by the segregated system.[21]

Leading up to the 1968 school year, many school boards sought to rely on "freedom of choice" plans as a response to the desegregation mandate. Under these plans, while all students were given a choice of which school to attend, Whites typically levied intense pressure and intimidation to steer Black families away from previously all-white schools, and practically no White families chose to attend previously all-black schools. Thus, the practical effect of such plans was to continue to perpetuate segregation. In 1968, in a challenge to the use of such plans, the Supreme Court held that the plan in question was insufficient to address the problem of segregation and that school boards must accept "the affirmative duty to take whatever steps might be necessary" to convert to a unitary system and to eliminate racial discrimination "root and branch."[22]

Nevertheless, intense resistance to desegregation continued. In 1969, in a consolidated case involving over 30 Mississippi school boards, Civil Rights Division attorneys pressed to eliminate and replace "freedom of choice" proposals with affirmative desegregation plans. In August of that year, the Fifth Circuit ruled that the new desegregation plans must be implemented by September. One week later, however, the Division's Assistant Attorney General sought to delay the new integration plans until the 1970 school year. In response to this change of position, career attorneys in the Division publicly protested.[23] Later that year, the Supreme Court issued a unanimous decision that the school districts must integrate without delay in the middle of the school year.[24] At that point, the Division resumed its efforts to actively pursue desegregation, and at the end of 1970 had undertaken a total of 214 active school cases.

---

[20] Title IX of the Civil Rights Act of 1964 allowed the Justice Department to intervene in private suits.

[21] *United States v. Jefferson County Board of Education*, 372 F.2d 836 (5th Cir. 1966), adopted en banc, 380 F.2d 385 (5th Cir. 1966)—immediate desegregation for all states of the 5th Cir., 417 F. 2d 834 (5th Cir. 1969); see also *United States v. Montgomery County Board of Education*, 395 U.S. 225 (1969)—desegregation of faculty and staff required.

[22] See *Green v. New Kent County School Board*, 391 U.S. 430, 438 (1968).

[23] The United States Commission on Civil Rights also called this reversal a "major retreat in the struggle to achieve meaningful school desegregation." Cited in Appellee's Brief, 1969 WL 120225.

[24] *Alexander v. Holmes County Board of Education*, 396 U.S. 19 (1969).

In addition to challenging "freedom of choice" policies in the South, the Division attempted to desegregate Northern and Midwestern public schools[25] and challenged dual systems in higher education.[26] The Division's education work over the past 50 years, however, is not limited to securing public school desegregation. The Education Section has committed itself over the years to equal education for students with limited-English proficiency (LEP), to equal access for disabled students through enforcement of the Americans with Disabilities Act, and to equal opportunity for female students to participate in sports programs.

Since the closing of Prince Edward County schools in 1959, the region has made great strides towards integration and racial reconciliation. In 2003, the Virginia General Assembly passed a resolution apologizing for massive resistance, and in June 2003, Prince Edward County granted honorary diplomas to the students who would have graduated from R.R. Moton High School. Currently the largest public high school in the area, Prince Edward County High, is fully integrated with a population that is 56 percent Black and 43 percent White. T.C. Williams High School in Alexandria, while not constructed until after the Civil Rights Act of 1964, has also overcome significant resistance to integration. Though the city's public schools were desegregated in 1959, the three area high schools were consolidated and subsequently integrated in 1971 to remedy pervasive racial imbalances in the 1960s. While these school districts have made significant local progress, further protections by the Civil Rights Division are necessary nationwide, for schools are increasingly becoming resegregated.[27]

While the Justice Department committed to aggressive desegregation efforts in the late 1960s, those efforts have been consistently scaled back in subsequent decades. The courts have undermined progress in achieving racial equality and diversity by limiting possible remedies for segregation. In *Milliken v. Bradley* (1974), for instance, the Supreme Court blocked a desegregation plan in Detroit that relied on inter-district busing, ruling that dismantling a dual school system did not require any particular racial balance in each school. In rejecting inter-district busing and emphasizing the importance of local control over the operation of public schools, the decision exempted suburban districts from assisting in the desegregation of inner-city school systems. Limitations such as this sanction *de facto* segregation as a replacement for the *de jure* system outlawed by *Brown*.

Recent decisions such as that from the *Seattle* and *Louisville* cases, though continuing to endorse diversity as a compelling state interest, may undermine local school districts' voluntary strategies to combat segregation. The work of the

---

[25] *Reed v. Rhodes*, 607 F.2d 714 (6th Cir. 1979) (Cleveland, OH); *Liddell v. Bd. of Ed.*, 667 F.2d 643 (8th Cir. 1981)(St. Louis, MO); *United States v. Yonkers*, 837 F.2d 1181 (2nd Cir. 1989)(Yonkers, NY).
[26] *Ayer and United States v. Fordice*, 505 U.S. 717 (1992).
[27] Orfield, G., Eaton, S., and the Harvard Project on School Desegregation. *Dismantling Desegregation: The Quiet Reversal of Brown v. Board of Education*. New York: New Press, 1998.

Education Section of the Civil Rights Division, which contributed greatly in the early years to fuel the fire of integration, has stalled in recent years. It is the responsibility of the Civil Rights Division to contest efforts to scale back the federal government's promise to ensure equal protection and educational opportunity for all its students.

III. EMPLOYMENT DISCRIMINATION

We…are not interested in Negroes getting more work, Negroes have too much work already. What we want Negroes to get is less work and more wages.
A. Philip Randolph, "Our Reason for Being." March 1919[28]

Born in Karachi, Pakistan, but living in the United States since he was one year old, New Yorker Mohammad Salman Hamdani was equally proud of his Muslim heritage and American citizenship. On September 11, 2001, it was believed that the 23-year-old part-time ambulance driver and police cadet heard about the terrorist attack on his way to work and rushed over to help. Unfortunately, his whereabouts that day remained unconfirmed until 2002 when his remains were positively identified at the World Trade Center site. "A compassionate, warm-hearted young man," says Salman Hamdani's mother, his "greatest desire in life was to help others."[29]

The terrorist attack on September 11, 2001, was a singular act of horror not seen on U.S. soil since Pearl Harbor. The quick response of New York City firefighters, law enforcement officers, and medical workers like Mohammad Salman Hamdani to the tragedy made them heroes. These officers – men and women of all races and ethnicities – are the best that New York has to offer. They risked their lives for others and did so with honor.

Fifty years ago, many of these local heroes would not have had the opportunity to serve their city and their country as first responders. The doors to professions such as law enforcement and firefighting were all but locked in 1957 to people of color. Fire stations were notoriously segregated in the days preceding the civil rights movement. In San Francisco, for instance, there were no black firefighters at all before 1955 and women were not allowed to apply before 1976. [30]

Too often, in the 1950s and 1960s, Blacks were relegated to lower paying and less desirable jobs, and were excluded by many traditionally "white" industries and professions – particularly in the South. In many manufacturing industries, for example, Blacks held the jobs that were more physically strenuous, and often hotter or dirtier, while only Whites could compete for better paying supervisory positions. To make matters worse, unions at the time boasted many restrictions and employment hierarchies. Women were also relegated to low-paying jobs, thus earning about half that of men in 1960.

---

[28] Randolph, A. Philip. "Our Reason for Being." First editorial of *The Messenger*, March 1919. Available at: http://historymatters.gmu.edu/d/5125/

[29] U.S. Department of State's Office of International Information Programs. *September 11: Victims and Heroes*. Available at: http://usinfo.state.gov/albums/911/homepage.htm.

[30] Yi, M. "Minorities Named to Key Posts at SFFD." *Examiner*. 26 July 2000, A1; Available at: http://sfgate.com/cgi-bin/article.cgi?file=/examiner/archive/2000/07/26/NEWS11839.dtl

Much of the change that we have seen in employment with respect to racial and gender discrimination can be directly attributed to the Civil Rights Division's enforcement of Title VII of the Civil Rights Act of 1964, which prohibits discrimination in employment based on race, sex, religion and national origin.[31]

Initially, few cases were brought following under Title VII. At that time, the Equal Employment Opportunity Commission (EEOC), created by the 1964 Civil Rights Act, had no enforcement authority. It could only investigate, conciliate, or refer cases to the Justice Department to litigate. A few years later, the Civil Rights Division put employment litigation on its priority list, filing six discrimination suits in the summer of 1967 and another 26 in 1968. At issue in the early employment cases was whether Title VII prohibited only purposeful discrimination or whether it also prohibited practices that appeared to be neutral but had a discriminatory effect.

The Justice Department first raised this issue in suits challenging union hiring practices. In one suit, an all-white asbestos workers union restricted membership to sons (or nephews raised as sons) of union members. Without union membership, individuals could not get hired in the insulation and asbestos trade. A second suit challenged a seniority system that perpetuated the effects of past discrimination. Both practices – restricted union membership and the seniority system – were ruled unlawful under Title VII by lower federal courts.[32] The Supreme Court addressed the issue of discriminatory hiring practices in 1971, after a divided Fourth Circuit ruled that Duke Power could require new hires for previously all-white jobs to have a high school degree and pass a written "ability" test. The Justice Department supported the plaintiffs in the case, noting that Duke Power's new hiring criteria were neither expected of previously hired White employees nor necessary to fill the job description.[33] The plaintiffs prevailed unanimously in the Supreme Court, which held that facially neutral "practices, procedures or tests that are discriminatory in effect cannot be used to preserve the 'status quo' of employment discrimination."[34]

In 1969, the Division sought back pay for the first time in an employment discrimination lawsuit. The Justice Department also determined that the affirmative action practice of requiring numerical goals and timetables for hiring

---

[31] Also, Executive Order 11,246, issued by President in Johnson in September 1965, gave the Labor Department the responsibility of enforcing nondiscrimination for federal contractors and subcontractors.

[32] *Vogler v. Asbestos Workers 53*,   (E.D. La. 1967); *United States v. Local 189 United Papermakers*, 282 F. Supp. 39 (E.D. La. 1968).

[33] See *Griggs v. Duke Power*, 401 U.S. 424 (1971).

[34] *Vogler, supra* note 32, at 430. "The Act proscribes not only overt discrimination but also practices that are fair in form, but discriminatory in operation. The touchstone is business necessity. If an employment practice which operates to exclude Negroes cannot be shown to be related to job performance, the practice is prohibited. ... [G]ood intent or absence of discriminatory intent does not redeem employment procedures or testing mechanisms that operate as 'built in headwinds' for minority groups and are unrelated to measuring job capability." *Ibid*, 431.

could be required for federal contractors as part of Executive Order 11246, which prohibited discrimination based on race, national origin, or religion by employers with federal contracts. The Division included goals and timetables in the relief and in settlements it sought in Title VII litigation. Following suits against Bethlehem Steel and United States Steel, the Division brought a nationwide suit against the entire basic steel industry in 1974, covering more than 700,000 employees at that time. A nationwide suit against over 250 trucking companies was brought that same year, resulting in a consent decree with the employers. These suits combined "brought over two million employees under the coverage of consent decrees with goals, timetables, and back pay."[35] In the same vein, a case was brought against the Alabama Department of Public Safety in 1972, in which the district court found that there had never been a Black trooper in the 37 years of the state patrol. The court required a one-for-one hiring of Black and White troopers until the Department met a goal of 25 percent Black troopers.[36]

In 1974, the federal government reorganized Title VII enforcement and the litigation authority against private employers was transferred to the EEOC. The Division's Employment Litigation Section was tasked with aggressively enforcing the provisions of Title VII against state and local government employers. From 1975 to 1982, the Civil Rights Division brought cases covering recruiting, hiring and promotional practices of local and state governments, predominately against police and fire departments, which opened up their ranks to minorities and women.[37] Similar cases were brought against states and counties to include minorities and women in jobs in correctional institutions.

In 1978, the Civil Rights Division also worked with the EEOC and other agencies to issue the *Uniform Guidelines on Employee Selection Procedures*. These guidelines provided employers, labor organizations, and the courts with uniform federal guidance on what employers could and should do to create and implement hiring practices and standards that are non-discriminatory. These guidelines applied to federal government hiring as well.

The policies and practices of the Employment Section of the Division shifted dramatically under the Reagan Administration. In 1983, the Department filed an *amicus* brief in a private suit against the New Orleans Police Department, arguing that no affirmative action remedies – including race conscious measures

---

[35] Rose, D. "Twenty-Five Years Later: Where Do We Stand on Equal Employment Opportunity Law Enforcement." *Vanderbilt Law Review*, Vol. 42, May 1989: 1122, 1145.

[36] *NAACP and United States v. Allen*, 340 F. Supp. 703 (M.D. Ala. 1972). Later, the District Court ordered a similar race-conscious requirement for promotions to higher ranks, and the Supreme Court upheld the relief in 1987 despite the United States' reversal of position and opposition to the remedy. See *United States v. Paradise*, 480 U.S. 149 (1987).

[37] See *United States v. City of Alexandria*, 614 F.2d 1358 (5th Cir. 1980) (covering 45 municipal police and fire departments in Louisiana), and *Vulcan Pioneers, Inc. v. New Jersey*, 832 F.2d 811 (3rd Cir. 1987) (covering 12 fire departments in New Jersey). Cases were brought during this time against state police agencies in Florida, Maryland, Michigan, New Hampshire, New Jersey, North Carolina, Vermont and Virginia.

– are lawful to correct past discrimination under Title VII except those that assist individual and specific victims of discrimination. The Fifth Circuit rejected that position.[38] However, in 1984 the Division began systematically revising its consent decrees with over 50 public employers that had required affirmative action remedies, to eliminate numerical goals. As one commentator put it, "[t] he cumulative effect of the Justice Department's positions was that the lawyers for the executive branch, who had been in the forefront of advocating the civil rights of blacks, other minorities, and women since the days of President Truman, became the advocates for a restrictive interpretation of the civil rights laws."[39]

One area in which the Division *did* continue equal employment enforcement during the 1980s was in residency requirements. In 1983, the Division brought suit against the city of Cicero, Illinois, for requiring applicants for employment to live in the city. Because the city was over 99 percent White, the city work force was all White. Twelve similar suits followed in other white suburbs of Chicago. The court ruled that the residency requirements violated the disparate impact standard of *Griggs v. Duke Power*, and settlements or summary judgments were entered in all 13 suits. Lawsuits against 18 suburbs of Detroit were also successful.

In the 1990s, the Civil Rights Division renewed its efforts to enforce Title VII against public employers through "pattern or practice" cases and individual cases referred by the EEOC. The Employment Section also took on a critical role in defending the federal government's affirmative action programs. In July 1995, President Clinton confirmed that the federal government would "mend, not end" affirmative action and ensure that federal programs were consistent with the Supreme Court's new, more rigorous, standard for evaluating whether such programs were constitutional.[40] The Justice Department subsequently undertook a meticulous review of all federal programs to ensure their fairness, flexibility, and constitutionality.

In recent years, prosecution of employment cases by the Division has been drastically reduced. A review of the Division's enforcement activity in recent years reveals a considerable decline in the number of Title VII lawsuits being undertaken, particularly as related to the issue of "disparate impact." The Division must consider these cases a higher priority, as they seek systemic reform of employment selection and promotion practices that adversely affect the employment opportunities of women and minorities. Strong evidence suggests that the problem of systemic employment discrimination persists, and because these cases are complex and difficult, the Justice Department is oftentimes the only entity that can successfully intervene.

---

[38] *Williams v. New Orleans*, 729 F. 2d 1554 (5th Cir. 1984).
[39] Rose, *supra* note 35, at 1155, 1157.
[40] See *Adarand Constructors v. Pena*, 515 U.S. 200 (1995).

IV. FAIR HOUSING

MAMA: *'Course I don't want to make it sound fancier than it is…It's just a plain little old house – but it's made good and solid – and it will be ours…*
RUTH: *Where is it?*
MAMA: *Well – well – it's out there in Clybourne Park – …*
RUTH: *…Mama, there ain't no colored people living in Clybourne Park…*
MAMA: *…I just tried to find the nicest place for the least amount of money for my family…Them houses they put up for colored in them areas way out all seem to cost twice as much as other houses. I did the best I could.*
Lorraine Hansberry, *A Raisin in the Sun*[41]

Even though the housing boom has cooled and the downturn in the subprime market is rippling through the credit markets, home ownership continues to sit at the heart of the American dream. For many prospective homeowners today, the chief concern is whether they can afford their neighborhood of choice or whether they should take out a fixed or variable rate loan.

Fifty years ago, however, many families across the country faced much graver challenges to homeownership than we consider today – whether their houses would be bombed upon moving in. This happened to Percy Julian – the famed African-American chemist – when he and his family moved into Oak Park, Illinois, in 1950. The Julian home was fire-bombed on Thanksgiving Day just before they moved in. The attacks galvanized the community, which supported the Julians; but for years afterward, father and son often felt compelled to watch over their property by sitting in a tree with a shotgun.

In 1968, Congress responded to mounting evidence of intractable housing discrimination by enacting the Fair Housing Act. The Act prohibits both public and private discrimination on the basis of race, color, religion, and national origin in the sale and rental of housing. For the first time, it also allowed money damages to be collected in Justice Department suits.

The Civil Rights Division quickly applied this new authority, and a number of its first cases resulted in negotiated consent decrees. Developers of residential housing and owners and managers of urban rental apartments agreed to use objective, nonracial sales and rental criteria, as well as to engage in affirmative marketing efforts to seek minority customers. One of the first litigated cases resulted in similar affirmative relief.[42] Other early cases involved racial steering, in which real estate agents only showed minority applicants apartments or houses in areas that were already predominantly occupied by people of color. High profile cases were brought against Chicago real estate agents, Fred and Donald Trump in New York City, and the owners of the LaFrak housing complex – also in New York City

---

[41] Hansberry, L. *A Raisin in the Sun*. New York: Random House Inc., 1995, 76-77.
[42] *United States v. West Peachtree Tenth Corp.*, 437 U.S. 221 (5th Cir. 1971).

Another case of note involved the City of Black Jack, Missouri, just outside St. Louis. In 1969, a community organization in St. Louis began planning to construct multifamily apartments for low and moderate income residents in a predominantly Black area of the city. It found a location outside the city, in an unincorporated part of St. Louis County called Black Jack, which was already designated for multi-family units. When they learned of this plan, Whites in the area (Black residents made up less than 2 percent), successfully petitioned the county to incorporate as the City of Black Jack. They then enacted a zoning ordinance prohibiting the construction of any new multifamily dwellings. The Civil Rights Division challenged the zoning ordinance and the court ruled that the racial effect of the zoning ordinance was sufficient to violate the Fair Housing Act, and that the Division did not need to prove racial intent: "Effect and not motivation is the touchstone, in part because clever men may easily conceal their motivation."[43] Allowing the Division to focus on discriminatory effect rather than only intent empowered it to take on significantly more cases in recent years.

In 1980, the Civil Rights Division and the Yonkers branch of the NAACP filed suit against the City of Yonkers and the Yonkers School Board, charging that the city had engaged in systematic housing and school segregation for 30 years. This was the first case in which both school and housing segregation were challenged in the same lawsuit. After a three-month trial, the court found that the city had restricted housing projects to southwest Yonkers, a predominantly minority area, for the purpose of enhancing racially segregated housing and intentionally to limit minority children to schools with predominantly minority student bodies.[44]

In 1988, Congress enacted a Fair Housing Amendments Act that provided stiffer penalties, expanded the Act's coverage to include disabled persons and families with children, and established an administrative enforcement mechanism through the Department of Housing and Urban Development (HUD). The Act also required the design and construction of new multifamily dwellings to meet certain adaptability and accessibility requirements. With these amendments, the Division's Housing Section tripled; and in 1991, it established a fair housing testing program, wherein individuals pose as prospective buyers or renters to assess whether the housing providers discriminate. The Division generally uses both Black and White non-volunteers from other parts of the Justice Department as individual testers. From 1992 to 2005, the Division filed 79 pattern or practice cases using evidence from the fair housing testing program.

In the 1990s, the Division began its Fair Lending program. Discrimination in lending generally involves one of three types of issues; (1) marketing practices in

---

[43] *United States v. City of Black Jack*, 508 F2nd 1179, 1186 (8th Cir. 1975).
[44] *United States v. Yonkers Board of Education*, 624 F.Supp. 1276 (S.D.N.Y. 1985), aff'd, 837 F.2d 1181 (2nd Cir. 1987). As a remedy, the court ordered the City to provide for 200 units of public housing in white areas of the city, as well as to allocate its federal housing grants for several years in ways that would advance racial integration. It also ordered the school board to create magnet schools and implement a school assignment program furthering desegregation.

which the availability of loans depends on the racial or ethnic composition of neighborhoods (also known as redlining); (2) underwriting policies and practices in which lenders use different standards to assess the credit worthiness of applicants, and offer different levels of assistance to applicants based on race; and (3) pricing practices in which minorities and other protected groups are charged more for credit than other similarly situated borrowers.

The Department's first case related to underwriting practices, which was brought in 1992, stemmed from an *Atlanta Journal* series on the Decatur Federal Savings and Loan. Black and Hispanic applicants were rejected for mortgage loans in significantly higher proportions than White applicants. Bank employees also assisted White applicants with the loan process, but not Black applicants. A consent decree was entered that required fair lending training for loan officers, advertising and marketing to minority neighborhoods, and the creation of new branches in minority neighborhoods. In 1993, the Division settled with Blackpipe State Bank in South Dakota for redlining; the bank had refused to make secured loans to Native Americans living on Reservation lands. Loans to purchase cars, mobile homes, and farm equipment were simply unavailable to Native American borrowers. The bank that purchased Blackpipe agreed to set up a fund to compensate victims, to establish a marketing program and conduct financial seminars on Native American reservations, and to recruit qualified Native American applicants for job openings at the bank.

In 1994, the Division entered into a consent decree with Chevy Chase Bank, after it alleged that the bank was not marketing loans in predominantly African American neighborhoods of Washington, D.C. and Prince Georges County. Chevy Chase Bank agreed to pay $11 million to the neglected areas through a special loan program and through service efforts geared toward those neighborhoods. Other fair lending cases involved allegations of racially discriminatory practices relating to the sale of homeowners insurance (Milwaukee), discriminatory pricing (Brooklyn, Long Beach, CA), and predatory lending (New York City, Washington, D.C.).

The results of these efforts were remarkable in such a short period of time. Due in part to the Division's work and its general impact on the banking profession, the availability of loans to minorities expanded dramatically. At the same time, however, the Division has done little over the past 10 years to require conventional lenders to penetrate the African-American and Latino homeownership markets nationwide. It has failed to challenge the discriminatory predatory practices – such as steering Blacks and Latinos to subprime loans and lenders when they could qualify for conventional loans – that affect the lending market so dramatically today. Although indications of redlining in the homeowners insurance industry continue to surface, the Division has not been aggressive enough in recent years in confronting this discrimination directly or in correcting underlying practices.

Additionally, despite its promising start in addressing residential segregation based on race, the Division has not in recent years used its authority to address real estate sales discrimination and discriminatory zoning practices that exclude or limit housing opportunities for African Americans and Latinos. The loss of the Division's momentum in this area has left a significant vacuum in the efforts of the federal government to end residential segregation. This failure is particularly disheartening in the face of the Supreme Court's recent school desegregation rulings, which leave fair housing enforcement as one of the few remaining options to promote school desegregation.

The general criticisms of politicization, anemic enforcement, and a disregard of mission further affect housing discrimination enforcement, as they do with regards to other civil rights issues. The Fair Housing Act clearly states that the Division "shall" file cases investigated and charged by the Department of Housing and Urban Development. With increasing frequency, however, the Division has rejected responsibility for filing these cases – declining to conduct additional investigations or declining the cases altogether, thereby prolonging and duplicating the legal process. In one Chicago case, for example, the Division refused to file a federal suit after a referral from HUD. The Division stalled on the case for so long that Representative Jesse Jackson, Jr. requested that the Division investigate the case. The case was eventually settled, but the Division's delays undercut the promise of full enforcement of the Fair Housing Act, and thus the relief provided to the complainant in the case.

The number of enforcement cases brought by the Division – both "pattern or practice" and HUD election cases – has dropped significantly in recent years; and that decrease is most evident in cases alleging racial discrimination. The Division's fair housing testing program has been reduced, and the Division has not advanced a strong fair lending or homeowners insurance enforcement portfolio for years. Given both the problems evident in the subprime market and the persisting patterns of residential segregation, predatory lending and sales and zoning practices that discriminate based on race and national origin should be at the top of the Division's agenda. It is evident that the Division has not wielded its voice to the fullest extent in combating these injustices.

Unfortunately, as with many other sections of the Civil Rights Division in recent years, many qualified attorneys have left and/or been pushed out by the administration. A diminishing staff promises a loss of both institutional memory and familiarity with the Fair Housing Act, thus reducing the ability of the Section to get back on its feet. As homeownership continues to sit at the heart of the American dream, the Division must recommit itself to redressing these ongoing setbacks; for while minority home ownership has undoubtedly advanced over the last 50 years, it still remains out of reach for too many Americans.

V. PUBLIC ACCOMMODATIONS

All of Africa will be free before we can get a lousy cup of coffee.
James Baldwin[45]

Richard and Angela Edmond of Greenville, Mississippi are planning a summer vacation to Daytona Beach with their high-school-aged kids, Kevin and Marcus. Heading out on a Friday, they plan to spend a night in Selma, Alabama, to break up the drive and to have dinner with Mrs. Edmond's parents, the Hurstons. Having resided in Selma their whole lives, Mr. and Mrs. Hurston are well-known within their tight-knit neighborhood, particularly for their ongoing involvement in local civil rights issues. Over dinner, the family discusses the Hurstons' participation in the famous 1965 voting rights march from Selma to Montgomery and the voter registration drives they organized after moving back home from college. It doesn't take much to convince the grandkids to accompany them in the morning to see the A.M.E. Church where Dr. King spoke on voting rights in the 1960s.

On their way to the local Comfort Inn after dinner, the Edmonds are reminded of how differently they navigate public life in Alabama from their parents. Fifty years ago, they would not have been welcomed at most hotel chains in their area, nor would they have been served dinner in a racially integrated environment.

While pockets of injustice in customer service still exist throughout the nation, the law no longer supports them. Fifty years ago, segregation in public accommodations – particularly in the South – was the norm. Whether it was in restaurants, bars, movie theaters, buses, hotels, or drinking fountains, African Americans were routinely denied service and relegated in the social realm to second-class citizens. Through local efforts in the early 1960s, such as the sit-in movement in Greensboro, North Carolina, students and civil rights organizations alike forced the issue of segregation into the public arena. Over the course of a year and a half, the sit-in movement had attracted over 70,000 participants and generated over 3,000 arrests in the name of equal protection under the law.[46] As a result of these and other civil rights efforts, the Civil Rights Act, passed by Congress in 1964, included provisions outlawing discrimination in public accommodations.

Title II of the Act requires that restaurants, hotels, theaters, sales or rental services, health care providers, transportation hubs, and other service venues afford to all persons "full and equal enjoyment of the goods, services, [and] facilities" without discrimination or segregation. Consequently, federal law prohibits privately owned facilities from discriminating on the basis of race, color,

---

[45] Quoted in Kasher, S. *The Civil Rights Movement: A Photographic History, 1954-1968*. New York: Abbeville Press, 1996, 35.
[46] Carson, C., Garrow, D., Gill, G., Harding, V., and Clark Hine, D., eds. *The Eyes on the Prize Civil Rights Reader*. New York: Penguin Books, 1997.

religion, or national origin, and the Americans with Disabilities Act extends this provision to include disability. In 1964, including a directive to address segregation in public accommodations was particularly controversial because the 1883 civil rights cases held that equal protection under the law did not extend to privately owned and operated establishments and facilities. In order to pass Title II, Congress used its constitutional authority over interstate commerce to authorize its actions. The provision succeeded, therefore, due to Congress' ability to intercede in the buying, selling, and trading of services. The year the Act was passed, the Supreme Court upheld Title II as a constitutional application of the commerce clause in *Heart of Atlanta Motel v. United States*.[47] The Supreme Court also upheld the Act in a companion case regarding Ollie's Barbeque – a family owned restaurant in Birmingham, Alabama, that served barbeque and home-made pies.[48]

In the *Heart of Atlanta* and the *Katzenbach* (Ollie's Barbeque) cases, both the hotel and the restaurant, respectively, had brought declaratory judgment cases against the United States in an attempt to force the courts to declare Title II unconstitutional. The Department prevailed in these cases, after which it continued a vigorous enforcement program throughout the late 1960s. Subsequently, thousands of hotels, restaurants, bars, pools, movie theaters and transportation facilities were forced to integrate. Though these efforts were extensive, few cases went to trial and resulted in reported decisions, as the majority of defendants settled and agreed to change their patterns and practices of discrimination. Additionally, most of the public accommodations cases in which the Department intervenes originate as private suits.

While drastic changes in the administration of public services have occurred over the past 50 years, discrimination in public accommodations has weakened but not disappeared. In recent years, the Civil Rights Division has been involved in multiple cases alleging overt racial and ethnic discrimination. In 1994, the Justice Department sued Denny's restaurants for discriminatory service. In *U.S. v. Flagstar Corporation and Denny's*, the Division filed and resolved a Title II action in California alleging that the chain consistently required Black customers to prepay for their meals, ordered them to show identification, discouraged their patronage, and removed them from selected restaurants entirely. On the same day the Department filed a consent decree in the California case, six Black uniformed Secret Service officers assigned to protect President Clinton set out to have breakfast with 15 other officers and were discriminated against at a Denny's in Maryland. A private class-action suit was filed and won. In the California case, the Civil Rights Division entered into a settlement that provided approximately

---

[47] 379 U.S. 241 (1964).
[48] See *Katzenbach v. McClung*, 379 U.E. 294 (1964). The Supreme Court also applied the 1964 Act to Piggy Park drive-in barbeque restaurants in South Carolina. See *Newman v. Piggy Park Enterprises*, 390 U.S. 400 (1968). This secured the law's application in drive-in (rather than only in sit-down) facilities.

$54 million to 300,000 customers and required Denny's to implement a nationwide program to prevent future discrimination.

In 1999, the Division investigated the Adam's Mark Hotel chain for discrimination against African-American hotel guests in Daytona, Florida, during the city's Black College Reunion. The Division's settlement included compensation to the reunion attendees as well as a substantial contribution to Florida's historically black colleges to develop scholarships and cooperative education programs in hotel and hospitality management.[49] It was not until the Civil Rights Division filed a complaint against Satyam, L.L.C., which owns and operates the Selma Comfort Inn, that the management and employees officially promised to stop discriminating against African-American guests at their hotel. According to the complaint, employees charged Black guests higher prices than Whites, denied them equal access to hotel services and facilities, and consistently steered them toward the back of the hotel until the Department of Justice intervened in 2001.[50]

Cases such as this remind us that while the landscape of public life today is a far cry from life in 1957, substantial work remains to eliminate the pattern and practice of discrimination in public accommodations. The Division must continue to commit itself to aggressive civil rights enforcement in the area of accommodations so that all Americans are protected equally from the systematic denial of public services.

---

[49] See *U.S. v. HBE Corporation d/b/a Adam's Mark Hotels* (2000).
[50] See *U.S. v. Satyam, L.L.C. d/b/a Selma Comfort Inn, et al.* (2001).

VI. POLICING THE POLICE and PROSECUTING THE KLAN

You may have heard a radio news report which aired briefly during the days after the jury's acquittal of the policemen in the Rodney King beating case. The report stated that public officials of the judicial system of Los Angeles routinely used the acronym N.H.I. to refer to any case involving a breach of the rights of young Black males…N.H.I. means "no humans involved." By classifying this category as N.H.I. these public officials would have given the police of Los Angeles the green light to deal with its members in any way they pleased.
    Sylvia Wynter[51]

The beating of Rodney King by officers of the Los Angeles Police Department on March 3, 1991, captured on videotape and broadcast around the world, shocked America. The tape all but confirmed the officers' use of excessive force and exposed to the public longstanding racial tensions in Los Angeles, with which its residents were all too familiar. The state prosecution of the four officers involved resulted in a complete acquittal. Within hours, riots broke out across Los Angeles that left 55 people dead and over 2000 wounded. In light of what appeared to many to be a wholesale miscarriage of justice, the Civil Rights Division opened a new investigation and initiated a federal prosecution. On August 4, 1992, the same four officers were indicted on two counts of intentionally violating Mr. King's constitutional rights by the use of excessive force.

In the federal trial, there was a racially mixed jury, expert medical testimony regarding King's injuries, and a dismissal of the defense's use-of-force "expert." By prosecuting this case, the Civil Rights Division expressed a commitment to racial justice not shown in the state system. The two-month federal trial of the four Los Angeles police officers ultimately ended with the conviction in April 1993 of two of the four officers, Sgt. Stacey Koon, the supervising officer at the scene, and Officer Laurence Powell, the officer who had delivered the most number of blows to Mr. King. Both defendants were sentenced to 30 months in prison.

Fifty years ago, many people living under Jim Crow could not envision a legal system in which equal protection under the law would extend to all Americans. From the Civil War until the 1950s, lynching was accepted as a method of imposing law and order in the South and maintaining a social caste system. An anti-lynching campaign was gradually legitimized and supported by the NAACP through legal challenges, but the law continued to criminalize Black behavior.[52]

The Jim Crow system of *de jure* segregation in the South not only relegated Blacks to second-class citizens for whom voting, education, and housing rights were restricted; it also denied Blacks adequate government protection from the racial violence employed to maintain this caste system as the status quo. Black

---

[51] Wynter, S. "No Humans Involved: An Open Letter to My Colleagues." *Forum N.H.I.: Knowledge for the 21st Century*, Vol. 1, No. 1, Fall 1994: 42.
[52] Davis, A. Y. *Are Prisons Obsolete?*, New York: Seven Stories Press, 2003, 23.

codes, racist statutes, and government unwillingness to protect Blacks from impending racial violence allowed members of the Ku Klux Klan (KKK) to carry out a racist regime of public violence with impunity. Since local officials were not interested in prosecuting white-on-black violence, police officers could also avoid culpability for abusing the civil rights of Black residents.

The brutal murder of Emmett Till in the summer of 1955 exemplifies the extent to which southern extremists were able to preserve Jim Crow under the guise of law and order. During the initial period following the *Brown v. Board* decision in 1954, the South witnessed tactics of massive resistance that resulted in pockets of highly publicized racial violence. In 1955, fourteen-year-old Emmett Till, who traveled from Chicago to visit relatives in Mississippi, was viciously murdered and disposed of in the Tallahatchie River for whistling at a White woman. Although the crime was prosecuted by state authorities, the defendants were acquitted by an all-white jury after deliberating for just over one hour. Immediately following the acquittal, the defendants publicly and shamelessly admitted their guilt.[53] These and other murders persisted unabated.

In the early years of the Civil Rights Division, criminal cases were limited in number and had limited effect. While the Division had the statutory authority to prosecute police brutality, the legal systems in the South were not prepared to cooperate. From January 1958 to July 1960, the Division brought 52 prosecutions, but only obtained convictions in four cases and *nolo contendere* pleas in two others. As former Assistant Attorney General for Civil Rights Burke Marshall recalled, "the problem of police misconduct was totally beyond reach" because of little resources, no local cooperation, and total exclusion of minorities from grand juries and trial juries.[54] Consequently, the Division brought few prosecutions for police violence against civil rights volunteers during voter registration drives, sit-ins, and protests.[55]

Widespread publicity of the Freedom Summer bus rides in 1964, however, garnered national attention for the issue of racial violence in the South. On June 21, 1964, the brutal KKK murder of three civil rights workers in Neshoba County, Mississippi – James Chaney, Andrew Goodman, and Michael Schwerner – placed the issue of Klan violence, in particular, on the public radar. National outrage over these murders prompted President Johnson to order the FBI to find the perpetrators, and sparked a federal government commitment to respond to Klan violence.[56]

---

[53] Lawson, S.F., and Payne, C. *Debating the Civil Rights Movement, 1945-1968*. Lanham, MD: Rowman & Littlefield Publishers, Inc., 1998, 12.
[54] Vera Institute of Justice, "Prosecuting Police Misconduct: Reflections on the Role of the U.S. Civil Rights Division." *Vera Institute of Justice*, 1998. Available at: http://www.vera.org/publication_pdf/misconduct.pdf.
[55] See, Stewart, J. "NAACP v. The Attorney General: Black Community Struggle Against Police Violence." *The Social Justice Law Review* , Vol. 29, 2006.
[56] Lawson and Payne, *supra* note 54, at 30-31.

In December 1965, the Division obtained its first successful prosecution of a Klansman. It was the case of Viola Gregg Liuzzo, a White civil rights volunteer and mother of five, who was murdered by four KKK members after the 1965 march from Selma to Montgomery, Alabama. One of the Klansmen in the car with the shooters was an FBI informant, so the killers were arrested the next day. Because the KKK wielded considerable power, the state's prosecution of this case resulted first in a mistrial and then in an acquittal in the second state trial. The Civil Rights Division interceded to bring the case to federal court in Montgomery, Alabama, where it achieved its first ever conviction in a civil rights death case.

In 1967, the Civil Rights Division was able to prosecute and convict some of the Neshoba and Lauderdale County deputy sheriffs who were responsible for the murders of Chaney, Goodman and Schwerner. In 1968, Assistant Attorney General Stephen Pollak instructed Division attorneys to intervene more forcefully in police brutality allegations. Also In 1968, Congress broadened the scope of protection afforded by civil rights statutes by making it a crime to interfere by force or threat of force with certain federal rights (such as employment, housing, use of public facilities, etc.) because of someone's race, religion, color or national origin. This is commonly known as the federal hate crimes statute.[57] The impetus for the passage of the federal hate crime law was the assassination of Martin Luther King, Jr. on April 4, 1968.

Today, the Civil Rights Division's criminal prosecutions of police brutality cases remain an important tool to redress wrongful criminal conduct of law enforcement officers. After the Simi Valley, California, jury acquitted the officers who beat Rodney King in a 1992 state trial, the Division confirmed the importance of policing the police by prosecuting and convicting the officers in federal court under the federal statute. The Division's work to prosecute hate crimes has expanded over the years to include an increased number of successful prosecutions of Klansmen in the South and White supremacists across the nation who have engaged in racially motivated violence.

Nevertheless, while criminal prosecutions address individual police misconduct, they fail to hold police departments accountable for perpetrating rather than protecting against widespread civil rights violations. Efforts to create federal accountability for patterns or practices of violations of civil rights within state and local police departments were met with resistance for decades. In the late 1970s, a court determined that the Division did not have the authority to bring a civil lawsuit against the Philadelphia Police Department alleging systematic abuse despite widespread evidence of routine brutality, illegal actions, and racist behavior.[58] In 1994, however, in response to the Rodney King incident and subsequent L.A. riots, Congress authorized the Attorney General to bring civil

---

[57] 18 U.S.C. 245.
[58] *United States v. Citv of Philadelphia*, 482 F. Supp. 1248 (E.D. Pa. 1979).

actions against state and local law enforcement agencies for a "pattern or practice" of police misconduct.[59]

In January 1997, the Division brought its first enforcement action under its civil pattern or practice authority against the Pittsburgh, Pennsylvania, police department. The Division's investigation found a pattern or practice of officers using excessive force, falsely arresting, and improperly stopping, searching and seizing individuals and evidence of racially discriminatory action. As a result, the Division entered into a consent decree with the police department that spelled out a series of reforms to address its systemic problems. Similar cases were brought against police departments in Los Angeles, Washington, D.C., Detroit, Prince Georges County, Maryland, and Cincinnati, Ohio, as well as against the New Jersey State Police. However, the Division has not entered into a single consent decree or settlement for alleged violations of the civil police misconduct statute since January 2004.

The Division's anemic enforcement of police pattern or practice cases in recent years has weakened the Department's overall effort to protect civil rights and to help police departments identify practices that undermine their law enforcement work. Without the Justice Department opening new investigations, there is little impetus for police departments to police themselves.

---

[59] Passed as part of the 1994 Crime Act, the provision is 42 U.S.C. 14141. The types of conduct investigated include excessive force, discriminatory harassment, false arrests, coercive sexual conduct, and unlawful stops, searches or arrests.

RECOMMENDATIONS

The best way to solve any problem is to remove its cause.
Martin Luther King, Jr., *Stride Toward Freedom*[60]

Fifty years ago, the attempt to integrate Little Rock High School demonstrated the need for the federal government to finally say "enough" – enough of allowing the states to defy the U.S. Constitution and the courts, and enough of Congress and the Executive Branch sitting idly by while millions of Americans were denied their basic rights of citizenship. The 1957 Civil Rights Act and the creation of the Civil Rights Division were first steps in responding to a growing need.

For years, we in the civil rights community have looked to the Department of Justice as a leader in the fight for civil rights. As this report outlines, in the 1960s and 1970s, it was the Civil Rights Division that played a significant role in desegregating schools in the old South. In the 1970s and 1980s, it was the Civil Rights Division that required police and fire departments across the country to open their ranks to racial and ethnic minorities and women. It was the Civil Rights Division that forced counties to give up election systems that locked out minority voters; and it was the Civil Rights Division that prosecuted hate crimes when no local authority had the will.

In recent years, however, many civil rights advocates have been concerned about the direction of the Division's enforcement. Over the last six years, politics too often appears to have trumped substance and altered the prosecution of our nation's civil rights laws in many parts of the Division. We have seen career Civil Rights Division employees – section chiefs, deputy chiefs, and line lawyers – forced out of their jobs in order to drive political agendas.[61] We have seen whole categories of cases not being brought, and the bar made unreachably high for bringing suit in other cases. We have seen some outright overruling of career prosecutors for political reasons,[62] and also many cases that have been "slow walked" to death.

In order for the Division to once again play a significant role in the struggle to achieve equal opportunity for all Americans, it must rid itself of the missteps of the recent past, but also work to forge a new path. It must respond to contemporary problems of race and inequality with contemporary solutions. It must continue to use the old tools that work, but must also develop new tools when they don't. It must be creative and nimble in the face of an ever-moving target. The following are recommendations for a way forward.

---

[60] King, Jr., M.L. *Stride toward Freedom: The Montgomery Story*. New York: Harper, 1958.
[61] Savage, C. "Civil Rights Hiring Shifted in Bush Era: Conservative Leanings Stressed." *The Boston Globe,* 23 July 2006.
[62] Eggen, D. "Criticism of Voting Law Was Overruled: Justice Dept. Backed Georgia Measure Despite Fears of Discrimination." *The Washington Post*. 17 November 2005: A01; Eggen, D. "Justice Staff Saw Texas Districting As Illegal: Voting Rights Finding On Map Pushed by DeLay Was Overruled." *The Washington Post*. 2 December 2005: A01.

A. De-Politicize the Civil Rights Division

Perhaps the most troubling aspect of the change in the Division in recent years is the extent to which politics has driven its decisionmaking. Changes in Administration have often brought changes in priorities within the Division; but these changes have never before challenged so directly the core functions of the Division, nor has there ever been such a concerted effort to structurally alter the Division through personnel changes at every level.

The Division's record on every score has undermined effective enforcement of our nation's civil rights laws. It is the personnel changes to career staff, however, that are in many ways most disturbing – for it is the staff that builds trust with communities, develops the cases, and negotiates effective remedies. Career staff has always been the soul of the Division, and it is under attack.

The blueprint for this attack appeared in a *National Review* article in 2002. The article, "Fort Liberalism: Can Justice's civil rights division be Bushified," [63] argues that previous Republican administrations did not succeed in stopping the Civil Rights Division from engaging in aggressive civil rights enforcement because of the "entrenched" career staff. The article proposed that "the administration should permanently replace those [section chiefs] it believes it can't trust," and further, that "Republican political appointees should seize control of the hiring process" rather than leave it to career civil servants – a radical change in policy. It appears that those running the Division got the message.

To date, four career section chiefs and two deputy chiefs have been forced out of their jobs, including the long-serving veteran who was responsible for overseeing enforcement of Section 5 of the Voting Rights Act. The criteria for hiring career attorneys have become their political backgrounds instead of their experience in civil rights. Longtime career attorneys have left the Division in large numbers. The amount of expertise in civil rights enforcement that has been driven out of the Division will be difficult to recapture.

The Civil Rights Division must restore its reputation as the place for the very best and brightest lawyers who are committed to equal opportunity and equal justice. It is not a question of finding lawyers of a particular ideology. Rather, it is a recommitment to hiring staff who share the Division's commitment to the enforcement of federal civil rights laws. That is not politics; it is civil rights enforcement.

---

[63] Miller, J. "Fort Liberalism: Can Justice's civil rights division be Bushified?" *National Review*, Vol. 6, May 2002.

B. Promote Access to Voting

The mission of the Voting Section at the Civil Rights Division is to protect the voting rights of racial, ethnic, and language minorities, thus making it easier for them to access the political process. The voting rights movement was born of a need to promote access as a cure for decades of it being denied to racial, ethnic, and language minority citizens.

In their work to protect the rights of language minority voters through the enforcement of Section 203 of the Voting Rights Act, the Division has pursued a vigorous enforcement program. However, in recent years, the Division has more often used its enforcement authority to deny access and to promote barriers that prevent legitimate voters from participating in the political process. For example, the Division's failure to block the implementation of Georgia's draconian voter ID law – later deemed unconstitutional and characterized as a "modern day poll tax" by a federal judge – opened the door for states across the country to pass similar onerous laws. Strong evidence exists that requiring a photo ID as a prerequisite to voting disproportionately disenfranchises people of color, the elderly, individuals with disabilities, rural and Native American voters, and homeless and low-income people, who are far less likely to carry a photo ID. Up to 10 percent of the voting-age population does not have state-issued photo identification.[64]

Nevertheless, the Civil Rights Division has sent a strong message to states in recent years that the federal government will not challenge voter ID laws, no matter how restrictive and no matter what the impact on minority voters.

The Division has also recently rejected numerous requests from voting rights advocacy groups to enforce that part of the National Voter Registration Act (NVRA) which requires social service agencies to provide voter registration opportunities, despite substantial evidence that registration at social service agencies has plummeted.[65] At the same time, the Division has shifted its enforcement priorities to enforcement of voter purge provisions of the law, which in many cases – as in Florida in 2000 – denied the right to vote to thousands of legitimate voters who were taken off the rolls.

Moreover, the Division has pushed states to implement the Help America Vote Act (HAVA) in an exceedingly restrictive way. For instance, it advocates keeping eligible citizens off the voter rolls for typos and other mistakes in registration forms made by election officials.

---

[64] Weiser, W., Levitt, J., Weiss, C., and Overton, S. "Response to the Report of the 2005 Commission on Federal Election Reform," Brennan Center for Justice at NYU School of Law, 2005. Available at: http://www.brennancenter.org/dynamic/subpages/download_file_47903.pdf
[65] An Election Assistance Commission report from July 2007 concluded that many states continue to ignore the requirements of the NVRA that public assistance agencies offer voter registration to clients, and noted that enforcement of the law by the Division has been virtually non-existent.

Finally, the Department of Justice's voter integrity initiative, established in 2001 by former Attorney General John Ashcroft, has created unnecessary commingling between criminal prosecutors in the U.S. Attorneys' offices and Civil Rights Division attorneys. These efforts can, if done improperly, result in a chilling effect on the participation of minority voters in the political process, particularly in jurisdictions with a history of disfranchising racial and ethnic minorities.

Rather than promote schemes that deny equal opportunity for citizens to vote, the Civil Rights Division should vigorously pursue enforcement of the Voting Rights Act and other existing statutes, as well as (1) combat voter ID laws that have a disproportionate negative impact on racial, ethnic, or language minorities – like those passed by both the Georgia and Arizona legislatures; (2) ensure that states comply with the NVRA's access requirements, such as those that compel social service agencies to afford their clients opportunities to register and to vote, and confirming that those registrations are processed appropriately; and (3) reinforce the firewall that exists between the Criminal Division's work to combat voter fraud and the Civil Rights Division's efforts to promote voter access.

C. Enforce Fair Housing Laws

The United States Department of Justice's Housing and Civil Enforcement Section has the powerful authority to bring cases involving a pattern or practice of discrimination that violates the Fair Housing Act to federal court. In recent years that authority has been used infrequently to address significant patterns of discrimination based on race and national origin, and almost never to challenge deeply entrenched residential segregation.

Fresh attention is being paid to racial and ethnic segregation in housing because of the recent Supreme Court decision that refused to permit race conscious school assignment policies in Louisville and Seattle. Although the Court has, over the years, pointed to ending housing segregation as a key way to avoid racially and ethnically segregated schools, the Justice Department has been turning a blind eye. The federal government's chief fair housing litigation agency has repeatedly failed to challenge discriminatory housing practices that potentially or actually segregate neighborhoods, as well as other types of discriminatory practices that affect many people of color. Discrimination in real estate sales and racial steering, discrimination in lending that destroys neighborhoods, and discrimination in zoning and land use practices that exclude people of color or limit their housing opportunities all continue virtually unchecked by today's Justice Department.

The Division should develop, on its own or in conjunction with advocates and enforcers, cases that focus directly on the key causes and perpetuators of residential segregation: real estate sales discrimination, lending discrimination including discriminatory steering and predatory practices by lenders, homeowners and renters' insurance discrimination, and zoning and land use practices. Its testing program should expand to examine discrimination in sales and lending. Its pattern and practice authority should be used broadly to address segregative practices that cut across communities in the same way that its early cases, like its case against Black Jack, did.

The Civil Rights Division's Housing and Civil Enforcement Section has also suffered from the loss of many career employees over the past six years and has experienced internal turmoil similar to that which has made headlines in the Division's Voting Rights Section. Hiring choices should focus on the fair housing expertise of applicants and the need to build capacity to take on the more challenging and important task of addressing systemic discrimination in our communities and providing meaningful enforcement of all of protections that the Fair Housing Act offers.

D. Ensure Compliance with the Americans with Disability Act (ADA)

In 1990, Congress enacted the Americans with Disability Act (ADA), and the Disability Rights Section is now one of the largest sections within the Civil Rights Division. Since 1990, the Section has brought suits to remove architectural and other barriers and ensure access to public accommodations (including all hotels, retail stores, restaurants, and places of recreation) and public transportation for person with disabilities, litigated against state and local governments, certified state and local building codes to ensure compliance with the ADA standards for accessible design, and instituted an extensive mediation program to promote voluntary compliance with the ADA.

The disability rights activities of the Division have historically enjoyed bipartisan support under Attorneys General Richard Thornburgh and Janet Reno. In recent years, the Civil Rights Division launched a successful "ADA Business Connection" series of forums designed to bring together business leaders and disability advocates to build a stronger business case for accessibility and disability as a diversity issue.

Moving forward, the Department will need to show leadership in making the judicial and the executive branches of the federal government true models of how to conduct the business of justice and government in a manner that is accessible and welcoming for all people. The federal government can and should do more to measure its compliance with accessibility requirements and to address deficiencies on a systematic basis. Enforcement of civil rights requirements is especially needed in the areas of access to higher education and access to voting, as widespread noncompliance with accessibility requirements exists in both of these important areas. There is also a need for stronger leadership on the issue of access to long-term services in non-segregated settings for people with significant disabilities.

In recent years, the Supreme Court has questioned the history of unconstitutional discrimination against people with disabilities by the States and has whittled away at the scope of the protected class in the ADA. In the years to come, disability advocates look forward to strong leadership from the Department of Justice to help stem the tide of Supreme Court federalism that has restricted disability rights.

E. Combat Employment Discrimination

The importance of the Department of Justice to the effective enforcement of Title VII of the Civil Rights Act of 1964 cannot be overstated. It is the organization with the prestige, expertise, and financial and personnel resources to challenge discriminatory employment practices of state and local government employers. As a general rule, private attorneys and public interest organizations lack the financial and personnel resources to act as private "Attorneys General" in the Title VII enforcement scheme.

Combating discrimination against African Americans has remained a central priority of the Division through both Republican and Democratic administrations. Unfortunately in recent years, enforcement of Title VII's protections for racial and ethnic minorities has dramatically decreased. In fact, over the past several years, the Employment Section has chosen to devote precious resources to a number of controversial "reverse discrimination" cases on behalf of Whites. As long as race discrimination against minorities remains a sad, harsh reality in this country, battling the persistent scourge of workplace discrimination against minorities must remain a central priority of the Employment Section.

Similarly, throughout most of its history, the Employment Section has recognized and fought for appropriate use of race- and gender-conscious relief. In many cases, the Justice Department entered into consent decrees with race-conscious relief provisions aimed at eliminating the last vestiges of this country's shameful legacy of race discrimination. The Employment Section must support the continued use of constitutional affirmative action programs to remedy past discrimination and promote equal employment opportunity. The Supreme Court has given its stamp of approval to many forms of race-conscious measures, including remedial affirmative action programs. Yet, in recent years, the Employment Section has sought to abandon existing consent decrees that included race-conscious relief and has targeted other employers who attempt to achieve a diverse workforce. Such a change in position threatens to set back the progress that has been made since the passage of the 1964 Civil Rights Act.

As the face of discrimination has changed over the years, so too must the methods by which we attack discrimination. Though egregious forms of individual employment discrimination persist, we find much of today's discrimination buried in a gauntlet of more covert screening and hiring processes. These include but are not limited to psychological profiling, written cognitive ability tests, personality inventory assessments, polygraph examinations, background screens, criminal background histories, credit score evaluations, and physical ability tests. Even well-intentioned employers and supervisors must grapple with the very real issue of hidden bias. The Employment Section must be dedicated to rooting out discrimination even where unlawful bias takes a more subtle form. Title VII prohibits not only the type of discrimination that is evident through "smoking gun" proof of malicious intent; it also outlaws less overt types of discrimination that play out through facially neutral policies or practices that disfavor a particular group.

The Section must continue to use all of the enforcement tools in its arsenal to address these more subtle forms of discrimination. The most powerful of these tools is the authority to bring pattern or practice cases with the support of statistical evidence. As employers engage in questionable practices like conducting credit checks on applicants and abusing information contained in background checks, the Employment Section should be at the forefront of the effort to ensure that employers utilize valid selection procedures. At a time when discrimination based on sexual orientation in various states is on the rise, it is important for Congress to give the Civil Rights Division the authority necessary to enforce the Employment Non-Discrimination Act (ENDA).

The Employment Section is uniquely positioned to tackle widespread discrimination that affects large numbers of public employees. The Section must use its statutory authority effectively to combat the persistent problems of discrimination in the workplace. If the Section returns to vigorous enforcement of the law, it can regain its reputation as a true defender of civil rights.

F. Promote and Maintain Integrated, High Quality Schools

The Supreme Court's opinion in the Seattle and Louisville cases, which limits the discretion of local school boards to take the race of students into account in seeking to voluntarily achieve racially and ethnically diverse learning environments for students, makes the work of the Civil Rights Division's Educational Opportunities (EO) Section more crucial than ever before. At the same time, those decisions mean the EO Section must reorder its priorities in a few fundamental ways.

First, the United States remains a party in many desegregation cases where there continue to be outstanding orders requiring school districts to eliminate the vestiges of prior discrimination. Currently the Section appears to be seeking to have as many of those districts as possible be declared unitary. Now that it is clear that once declared unitary, as was the Louisville school district, a school district may be forced to dismantle student assignment zones and other policies used to foster integration, the Department needs to stop districts from being declared unitary until it is clear that even post-unitary status, the district will remain integrated. The presence of an ongoing desegregation decree gives a school district more tools at its disposal to eliminate the effects of segregation. The Department needs to evaluate how to use the decrees it has obtained to maintain integrated school systems.

Second, the Department now must devote significant resources to determining how to use its enforcement powers under Title VI of the Civil Rights Act to prohibit discrimination by entities receiving federal funds. Most Local Education Authorities (LEAs) receive some form of federal funding. While Title VI complaints go to the Department of Education for investigation in the first instance, the EO Section has a significant role to play in advising the Department of Education Office of Civil Rights on how to interpret and enforce Title VI, and the Department of Justice is the entity that should be litigating those Title VI cases where the Department of Education finds that a recipient of federal financial assistance has been operating in a manner that has a disparate impact on minority students. There are numerous policies by school boards that are ripe for investigation under the disparate impact regulations of Title VI, such as zero tolerance disciplinary policies, practices resulting in the overrepresentation and mistaken categorization of minority students as having learning disabilities, and under-representation in academically gifted programs. The EO Section can contribute significantly to ensuring that the government vigorously enforces Title VI of the Civil Rights Act of 1964.

Finally, the Educational Opportunities Section has, in the past, initiated a number of creative programs to foster integrated schools at the K-12 level – such as those investigating how desegregated housing patterns contribute to integrated educational opportunities – by working carefully with all stakeholders, LEAs, parents, teachers and local governments, The Section must continue to undertake these and other creative initiatives in order to assist those school districts that are willing to create diverse learning environments but are daunted by the Supreme Court's limits on their discretion. The Section is, in many ways, the last hope for parents and children who want to see fulfillment of our nation's commitment to equal educational opportunities for all. The Section must re-order its priorities to achieve this mission.

G. Prosecute Police Misconduct and Hate Crimes

In 1994, Congress passed 42 U.S.C. 14141, the police misconduct provision of the Violent Crime Control and Law Enforcement Act of 1994. The provision authorizes the Attorney General to file lawsuits to reform police departments engaging in a pattern or practice of violating citizens' federal rights. The Division also enforces the Omnibus Crime Control and Safe Streets Act of 1968 and Title VI of the Civil Rights Act of 1964, which together prohibit discrimination on the basis of race, color, sex, or national origin by police departments receiving federal funds.

Starting in the late 1990s, the Special Litigation Section began to conduct investigations and implement consent decrees and settlement agreements where evidence demonstrated a violation of the police misconduct statutes. The investigations addressed such systemic problems as excessive force, false arrest, retaliation against persons alleging misconduct, and discriminatory harassment, stops, searches, and arrests. The decrees require the police departments to implement widespread reforms, including training, supervising, and disciplining officers, as well as implementing systems to receive, investigate, and respond to civilian complaints of misconduct. The decrees have had a widespread impact and are being used as models by other police departments. The Section has also used its authority under the Civil Rights of Institutionalized Persons Act (CRIPA) to reform restraint practices in adult prisons and jails and to obtain systemic relief in juvenile correctional facilities.

In recent years, however, the Section has retreated in its enforcement of these important statutes. This rollback has resulted in less accountability on the part of police agencies and a retreat in efforts to ensure that law enforcement and integrity go hand in hand. Given the lack of enforcement of these statutes by the Department of Justice, it is more important than ever to amend 42 U.S.C. 14141 to allow for a private right of action to enforce the statute. In addition, the Department needs to support an expansion of its authority, as outlined in the End Racial Profiling Act (ERPA). ERPA builds on the guidance issued by the Department of Justice in June 2003, which bans federal law enforcement officials from engaging in racial profiling. It would apply this prohibition to state and local law enforcement, close the loopholes to its application, include a mechanism to enforce the new policy, require data collection to monitor government progress toward eliminating profiling, and provide best practice incentive grants to state and local law enforcement agencies to enable them to use federal funds to bring their departments into compliance with the bill. The Justice Department guidance was a good first step, but ERPA is necessary to "end racial profiling in America," as President Bush pledged to do.

Moreover, while the Civil Rights Division has committed to vigorously enforcing the federal hate crimes statute, the statute itself is flawed. To strengthen its effectiveness, unnecessary obstacles to federal prosecution must be removed and authority must be provided for federal involvement in a wider category of bias motivated crimes. For instance, we have seen a rise in recent years in the number of hate crimes perpetrated due to discrimination based on sexual orientation. To enhance the federal response to this growing crisis, the Civil Rights Division must have the authority to prosecute *all* violent crimes based on race, color, religion, national origin, gender, sexual orientation, and disability. Expanding the authority needed to prosecute such cases is critical to protecting members of these groups from this most egregious form of discrimination.

CONCLUSION

If Congress lacks the authority to remedy discrimination, if states cannot be sued in federal court when they discriminate, and if federal agencies do not vigorously enforce the landmark laws of the 1960s, then civil rights protections lack the federal guarantee promised in the 14th and 15th Amendments.
                    Leadership Conference on Civil Rights Education Fund, 2003[66]

The 50th anniversary of the creation of the Civil Rights Division is a time to reflect on where we have been, where we are, and where we need to go in the struggle for civil rights and equal justice in America. We have undoubtedly come a long way – a very long way from racial violence, segregated lunch counters, poll taxes, and "Whites only" job advertisements. But we are not finished. Today, we face, among other things, predatory lending practices directed at racial minorities and older Americans, voter ID requirements that often have a discriminatory impact on minority voters, and English-only policies in the workplace; and so our work continues.

As this report confirms, one of the critical tools to our collective progress in civil rights has been the Civil Rights Division of the Department of Justice. And the heart and soul of the Division is and has always been its career staff. For 50 years, they have worked to help make our country what it ought to be: a place where talent trumps color and opportunity knocks on all doors; where you cannot predict the quality of the local school system by the racial or ethnic composition of the school's population; where access is a right, not a privilege; and where difference is both tolerated and valued.

We have concerns with the direction of the Civil Rights Division in recent years. Our hope is that the Division can meet those concerns with positive action for our future. This report begins to map out the way forward. We look forward to the continuing conversation.

---

[66] Leadership Conference on Civil Rights Education Fund. "The Bush Administration Takes Aim: Civil Rights Under Attack." *LCCREF*, April 2003, 9.